I0153228

"CAN YOU HEAR ME FROM THE HILLS AND THE MOUNTAINS?"

Sammy Pen

Willow Tree Books

Copyright © 2025 Sammy Pen

All rights reserved!
No part of this book may be reproduced, or stored in a retrieval system,
or transmitted in any form or by any means, electronic, mechanical,
photocopying, recording, or otherwise, without express written permission
of the publisher.

ISBN-13: 979-8-9997702-0-2

Printed in the United States of America

Dedication

Acknowledgement to my daughter, you have long admired my work for years snooping through my work. This book is dedicated to you with love and understanding forever and forever infinity and beyond the planet and stars align beyond a trillion years. May you never stop believing!

Acknowledgement and mention to my mother, who has inspired me through her own struggles to write my own pages. I thank you for holding onto decades worth of poems concealed in boxes and folders the world has yet to read and hear. You believed in me and kept my words till this very day.
Thank you!

Also, an acknowledgement to professor Steven Hobbs who was a light of inspiration when I forgot my own words and purpose in college at the age of 33 years old during his literature course. It's there I began writing again as an adult pursuing a higher education. He was my academic advisor and mentor who insisted on me pursuing an MFA Creative Fiction Writing degree. He saved me as a writer.
You are truly missed!

"I spent most of my life stuck inside a shell alone with my words, and it took decades to crack that shell. I have now stepped out to be seen and heard."

SAMMY PEN

"When one thing dies another thing is born. Perhaps, reinventing the self is part of letting the old go with death and the new self transforms from rebirth."

SAMMY PEN

CONTENTS

INTRODUCTION

The poems dives deep into the writer's obstacles, growth, self perseverance, self esteem, economic barriers, faith, feminism, social injustice and racism. This book of poetry explores the changes of the many seasons she has endured through growth and finding her purpose as a writer with adversity and her struggle as a black woman in America.

The poet is creating a platform in which she sees women as Queens who must realize that they are worthy, royal and earths' greatest contributors to the human population and society. Women can transform into their greater selves. Sammy wants those women to know that it is never too late to live your purpose and follow your dreams no matter how old and gray.

The poet was born and raised in the North East Bronx of New York City. She was born from parents who migrated to the states in the 1970's in their late teens from the island of Jamaica. She was raised culturally and adapted her parents practice, customs and beliefs as a first generation American.

She first discovered her love for poetry at the age of eleven years old, in which her teacher discovered her raw talent by confiscating her marble notebook. The teacher then called her a poet and then introduced her to poetry from Phillis Wheatley. Since then, her love of poetry grew.

She attended both elementary and middle school in the Bronx and attended high school in the city known as Manhattan, where she further explored poetry in creative writing and theater as her chosen art form of study. Some pieces of poetry from her high school era are within this anthology, along with copies of its original written work in this Hard copy edition never yet published until now. Sammy Pen has held on to them for more than twenty seven years.

The poet and writer like most young adults after graduating high school went straight into the workforce. She did not pursue a college degree or writing again until her early 30's, in which she earned her bachelor's degree in 2016 with a minor in Letters and a minor in Communications. She then went on to earn her Master's of Fine Arts in Creative Writing in Fiction in 2018 from the College of New Rochelle.

The poet tried building a career since her post graduation while raising her child as a single mother living in the Bronx of New York City. During her post graduation she was met with many obstacles and challenges. The poet managed to write during her post graduate experience and gather what has been well awaited by readers like you.

"Can You Hear Me From The Hills And The Mountains?"

By Sammy Pen

"Can You Hear Me From The Hills And The Mountains?"

"Can You Hear Me From The Hills And The Mountains?"

By Sammy Pen

Also Known as Sasha Mon Myrie

This is a collection of poems over the years well awaited because her voice no longer remains silent. She now utters the words once held captive in her mind now released to the eyes and ears of the unheard voices. This is for all the women out there desperately struggling to find their crown despite all the seasons in their lives. This is for all the women who have abandoned their dreams and desires and think it's too late to find and reinvent themselves. Let your voice be heard. This is for all young black and brown women who have endured racism, injustice, insecurities, and my black and brown teens finding their self identity and their purpose in life and for those of us who have contemplated an end but still manage to hold onto this precious life. They too must overcome the odds to achieve success, just keep fighting and believe you will succeed. Never give up, never.

While you don't have to be black, brown or a female to read and appreciate these words. You just need to be human because we all hurt and need to overcome our challenges in this life. Humans are faced with seasons no matter the race, ethnic, religion and gender.

Intro Poem

"A Writer Within, A Voice That Speaks"

Chapter 1 "Girl Speak"

"LITTLE GIRL SPEAK"

"THE LAST SHEET OF THE CHAPTER"

"SUICIDIE, MANY WAYS TO DIE"

"Alone in My Bedroom"

"Strong"

"IDENTITY"

"UNBREAKABLE"

Chapter 2 "Chapters"

"SEASON'S"

"Fight"

"My Song"

"Go Tell It!"

"WRITER"

"Speak"

"SPOKEN WORD"

"Here"

"MY WORDS"

"Shout"

"Psychic"

Chapter 3 "Black Spaces"

"Black Holes"

"Black Skins"

"To Live"

"Underscore"

"Ring for Liberty"

"Skin"

"Case"

"Labor"

"Run Run Run"

"Riches"

"SLUMBER BODIES!"

"Injustice Done to Me"

"Fighting"

"Worn Out"

"My Spirit Not Broken"

"Free Me"

"Night"

"The New Rising of Order"

"My Hope for Tomorrow"

"Royal"

"Black Spaces"

Chapter 4 "Her Dying Love and Sex Died With Him"

Chapter 5 "Conversation With God"

Chapter 6 "Steps to God, Steps to Her Crown, She is a Queen"

"Women Are Gods"

"DEAR QUEEN"

"CROWN HER YOUR GLORY"

"Crown"

"King"

"Trees"

"Fire"

The Last Chapter "Star"

"A Writer Within, A Voice That Speaks"

I am the voice that speaks within,

I am a writer that yearns to be heard,

A voice that burns to rise against the times of silence,

I am the coming of times, The Maya Angelou's rebirth,

I am the candle who lights the dark where the heart and mind reveals through pen and paper,

I am the writer of this piece who desires to craft the true gift of art,

I am the Phillis Wheatley, who discovered the art that was ordained from the beginning of birth,

I am the night owl who sees the beauty of the world even in the dark,

No longer do my hands suffer my burning to write these words on paper,

You see I suppressed my dreams and built my fears and silenced my voice,

I shall rise in the midst of my dreams where I was destined to rise,

I say thank you, Hughes, Maya, Alice and James,

Such great voices that has solely inspired me to write like the great of all times,

A poet, writer, and author, of all times

CHAPTER 1

"Girl Speak"

LITTLE GIRL SPEAK

I remember 27 years ago and how I felt.

I was frustrated with how I saw the world and girls like me didn't stand a chance.

I was 18 years old wearing a third eye that bore weight on me.

The truth was bitter, cold, rough and unchanged that it kept flirting with death.

18 and my dream was to die.

Just die.

I wanted to end my life because I saw no hope in the end.

I knew there were going to be struggles in my life.

Like foreseeing the future.

Dark days that rarely shed light.

I can not escape.

I tried to pray for brighter days.

I tried placing rainbows in my life.

I planted daisies but they all died.

I called that man but still no answer.

So 27 years later I am that little girl whose pain comes from the world in which she sees.

These are collections of poems written by me in my younger formative years as a teen, and as a young adult seeing the world in my view as I had dug deeper to see my reflection, my environment and who I was becoming or was. Poetry was my passion, my love, my sacred place. Expressing my thoughts, opinions and knowledge through a timeless piece of art.

These poems were written in the late 1990's when our environment helps shape and form our character and thought process. These poems have never been published before and have been safe for more than 27 years a bit faded as time progresses but its words are timeless and therefore, its original unedited and unrevised pieces are attached to the hardcover edition book.

"THE LAST SHEET OF THE CHAPTER"

Written March 3rd 1998 By Sasha Myrie

This is my last sheet called white paper
Expressed words riddled and rhymed
And written down before my eyes
The little girl has ended a chapter
A chapter to a new life and wonder
Yet the words which accumulate
Into gripping expressed feelings
Has now become a memorabilia
Something to adjust in about 6 years
To look back on a skilled writer
If i didn't get recognition
Now I will because it's my turn
Don't look back, Don't be afraid
That's what they tell you and I
So that all that has caused us pain
Will stop and begin a new chapter
But in every chapter there is a fear hidden behind the expressed words
Criticism by those who read and read with little understanding
This is my last sheet of this chapter

Revised on May 26th 2025

"SUICIDIE, MANY WAYS TO DIE"

Written March 16th 1998 By Sasha Myrie

Suicide, imaginative thoughts
Compresses to a victim
Why thoughts creeping in my mind
So many ways to die, Choosing one
Images popping up from everywhere
Young black and suicidal
Why?
Who's responsible?
The government's conspiracy
To entertain the youths
Telling them to recruit in an army suit
Now you got young brothers thinking that or gun activity been today's youth
Tired of seeing young brothers spreading dicks licking chicks clicks
Negroes don't understand the manifestation of a killa disease
One juke and up down with luke
The black race extinct
Younger and younger
Alive

Edited, and revised May 26th 2025.

"Alone in My Bedroom"

Written March 16th 1998

Alone in the world without anyone
Could you imagine yourself coming home to nothing to hold you?
Alone Like I've always been
It's like a dying seed that thirsts for water in order to grow
Instead it gives up hope and dies tomorrow
Being alone seems like the end for me
It seems like a dessert without cactus to look upon its majestic wonder
Sometimes I cry until it is unbearable
Alone in my sheets imagining a man's body beside me
I wake up in the morning to realize it was only a dream
I wish it was reality
Sometimes I wonder will you call me
Sometimes it seems I hear my name
By someone I used to love and now it becomes faded memories
If you could see the anger the reaps inside my soul
You would see the pain you've caused
And that I'm on my own
It seems as if I cared to remember the hateful words
That lingered in my mind each day........

Revised and edited on May 26th 2025
Part of this poem has not been published by the author.

"CAN YOU HEAR ME FROM THE HILLS AND THE MOUNTAINS?"

"Strong"

Originally written February 3rd 1997

As I look at the clouds in the morning gray
Wishing the sun would shine
Seeing the many faces of different races and ethnics on the train
The morning glow that becomes morning night leaves a shadow
Hidden beyond recognition
Because no one knows where to seek it
A life a battle to every child who has faced
May you be strong and hopeful
Where the many bridges failed and burned
There comes a river you may swim
As time dictates itself the repeated lines
These of our time will know that the next generation will know
our fears
If the clouds ever gave light
Then we may see things lightened

Edited on May 26th 2025

"IDENTITY"

Originally written February 11th 1998

This little child cried that night through as her tender body
ached through
Her shattering pain she suffered
There she sung a song of sad memories of her wicked past
As she looked into the wicked cold night
She cried but none heard her

"Oh mama, oh mama what have they done to me?"
"I'm striped of my pride"
"Why is my skin so dark and no one notices me?"
"They call me words obscene and discreet"
"Things a child should not know at this tender age"

"Oh mama, oh mama what have they done to me and my pride?"
"They tell me my nose is round and my lips are big and that no
man will ever love me because of my appearance"
"Then they tell me not even my own kind wants to deal with me"
"They tell me my thighs are too big and my butts too fat"
"They laugh and stare at me"

"They tell me I'm no good and will never be"
"They tell me my hair is too nappy"
"They tell me I'm dumb and ain't no one"
"Oh mama if you knew that this child was me and that these
indescribable words, hurtful wicked ignorant words came from"
"It hurts bad"

Revised May 25th 2025.

"UNBREAKABLE"

Originally written on March 3rd 1998

Break me down through the eyes of a child miraculously with shame and dignity
Did you think I'd fall like the Shang dynasty
No I stand

That's what you wanted me to do
Fall and sweep while sores would form
I've passed harder trials and tribulations

Every corner I've turned you've been standing there waiting for me to trip
I was built strong like pyramids in Egypt
Made from the hands of Gods
It would take more than that to kill me slowly and dreadfully

If you are trying to take me out
Kill me with a knife
But still if I live you could not break me

You look in my face with fear and hope for me to drop
But I will achieve my goals
Did you think I wouldn't make it?
You made me strong instead of weak
I face evil everyday in the eye
When they turn they laugh and hope for me to cry
Have you ever felt a stone so cold become weak and useless
No, because they've fought wars between men

I may not be smart and well educated
But I have knowledge and is wise
I'm human like all mankind
I will not break, shatter, cripple or fall
You will only make me strong
So I say "Thank you"

Edited, revised on May 27th 2025

CHAPTER 2

"Chapters"

"SEASON'S"

Can the child within my heart rise above?
Can I sail through the changing ocean tides?
Can I handle the seasons of my life?

Can I fight this wretched cold world and hold my head high?
Can I make it through the storms and hold the faith?
Can I get through the hurricanes and testify to my survival?

Can I weather the storms of my life and still hold the light?
Can I bear the heat wave and remain cool?
Can I sail the ocean and reach the shore?

I've got to make it through these seasons of life because only the
strong survive
I've got to brace for better days
I've got to pull my boots and rebuild better than before

It's okay to fall and rise every story has a story
It's okay to start
It's never too late to enter another season

I was thinking one day, and all of my emotions poured onto a journal. The struggle I faced became a mere reality of my life. The odds have been against me but somehow I thought to myself, I must gain the strength to fight. Written January 29th of 2018.

"Fight"

Fight with me,

Rise with me,

This war is about life,

Front and center,

Shield and armor,

There is no mercy,

There is no peace,

Life is not perfect,

The odds and obstacles constantly at my feet,

Somehow, I must and will conquer all that is against me,

My eyes have seen the glory,

My eyes have seen the light,

My eyes have seen the victory that now awaits the trophy……

"My Song" "

My song ain't no surprise

At a young age it was already compromised

The rhythm was never sweet

The melody always made me cry

I would never dance for joy

I could never sing those notes I hate so much

My song ain't no surprise for me

After one beat another would follow like a throbbing pain I just wish to rid of, I swear

Hit after hit I wish it would miss

It would sting in your ears

Then leaving a tune in your head

Something you didn't like but it stuck around like a bad hook

My song ain't no surprise

Other girls had a favorite song

I had none to claim

Truth is all the songs I knew made me cry

Not one to cherish

Too many beats after beats

My song ain't no surprise

Every time I heard a track play I would get sick to my stomach and everything I consumed was disposed of

My body began to feel the pain

Slowly, one step, two steps, three steps trying to feel my feet

My screams high like soprano

My song ain't no surprise

They gather in tons to witness my song, center stage at a stadium

Overwhelmed, shaken, fear sets in

The emotional scars that will forever play

No applause, no uncord please

My song ain't no surprise mama

Sad, hopeless, and heart broken

It's that song that airs on the radio and you hum to the tune despite the feelings built up inside

No wonder the feelings are still attached

Bringing back old shagged memories

I just wish I had happier songs to sing

Truth is their dark and potentially meaningless.....

It's a one hit wonder, no comeback or replay

It's this song I sing, and it makes me wonder will I ever live to sing the whole song sung

Go Tell It!

Life is never easy when you are fighting a battle
A battle that has left nothing but trauma
I rise from the ashes and from this world
My soul

I step off without self pity
Who am I?
A warrior whose life has been filled with battles
A soldier whose life has overcome many fights

A goddess who still owns her position in a world that hasn't
acknowledged her position
A god in control of her destiny
A destiny that must fulfill its purpose till the end of this life
Constant disappointments

Major setbacks
Pools of tears
Years of fear
Don't feel sorry dear

My life
My story
A circle in which I'm entangled
Go, Go, Go tell it on the mountain

He hasn't heard my screams
An echoing nightmare
Black girl, teen, woman, Queen
It's been the same team

With the same fight all my life
Black in the Bronx
Black in NYC
Black in America

Dreaming Mama Africa

Where is home?
I need you to rescue me
Poor I was born and maybe when I die
Destined

"WRITER"

I never chased fame or fortune because my dreams have been like pennies

Shinny and exciting but still poor, no value

I always buried my words and covered my soul

To bare my words for the world to see

Is setting my soul on fire

It burns not to reveal

It yearns to be free

Sometimes my mind is crippled from words that no longer unfold

My fingers feel numb because they haven't been moved to the muse

My voice silenced by fears

But deep within the need to hear my name

Where stories are told

And words heal the soul

And dreamers dream again

Where desires burn again

And what was lost is now found

All I ever needed was pen and paper

Words written

Words spoken

The world listening

The writer, the author, Sammy and Pen

"Speak"

Can you feel my rage
I shout from mount everest only the wind can hear my cry
The rage boiling inside of me 450 degrees I bleed pain and grief
43 years I've held my silence because I ask no pity for me
God I've beg your ears, hear my cry oh God from the top of the
world
I can't keep the silence inside anymore
Shout
Scream
From the top of the mountain this is my story
Please be kind to my words
Sacred and tucked away
Courage now to let my voice speak
Years as a prisoner in my own mind
World
In the hole alone
Naked and afraid all these years
Let me speak these words I've never told a soul
I am only human
Release
Release this pain
Release this pain now
Speak
Speak
Speak now,
From every hill, valley, streams, river, caves and mountain,
Shout
Shout on top of the world
Loud and clear
Speak now.

"SPOKEN WORD"

I am a God my eyes see the glory and darkness of this world,
My pain and grief are heartbreak, shattered hopes and dreams for
my youth
The chains beneath my earth
We have borne the seed, offsprings
Many nations

My tears the sea of the world's that worship thee
I am light in their eyes
I am the voice that lifts a nation
I am the beat of the drums
They dance to my name

They chant for me, their tongues utter my name
My presence before them makes them bow before me
Centered on stage
I am that light in their eyes
I am that voice of hope

My words do not fade they penetrate minds
I am their leader
These are my people
Hear my voice
I am the voice of the unheard

My eyes have seen it's glory
I am a God a goddess, my children
This earth has been our fortress
We have given birth to a nation
The heavens have blessed our vagina

"Here"

I have been through the storms and gutters of my many seasons
I have seen so many things that I still believe he covers me
Remembering the times I could not imagine the changes of life
I'm here to tell the story

I could not find my voice
I didn't know how to tell my story
I didn't think the skies would open up for me
I abandoned my pen and paper

I had to find my writer's voice
I had to find my words bottled up inside my mind
I had to out the flames and reignite
Silence each syllable then say it out loud

Hidden in my mind
Trapped in a corner gathering dust
I had to open my mind
I had to open my books and free my words

Free my mind from all that had consumed me
Liberate my hands again like that little girl who dreamed of pen
and paper
Exonerate me from oppression
Release these pages to the minds who have been waiting

I will fight to break free
Free me from what was stacked against me
I will claim my crown and glory
I will claim what's due

"MY WORDS"

My word my word I promised my words

You gave me hope the way I pray my words give hope to the hopeless

I kept faith all these years that someday I would share my words to those who lost faith to believe that dreams come true

My words my words sharp like a sword I've fought many obstacles to pave the way

Maybe someday these words these words of mines will give others the mercy to see that they can't and won't give up

Your words gave me healing in times of questions and soothed me like a swaddled baby suckling to sleep

I never lost hope nor vision that this day would come to crown little girls who dreamed and still dream

My words my words will not fail nor perish

Legacy that will stay forever

Forever a writer

Forever a poet

Forever an author

The universe hears my name

They chant as I chant from the hills and the mountains

Loud and proud I say it all

I found my voice

Now hear me speak

Hear me clear

Hear me now

I once did not speak

My mouth opened wide

The universe heard my name

There is a God within me

A God within

Blessed is she the Queen

Blessed is she the God

Blessed is she the Goddess

Goddess of life

Goddess of truth

She shines bright

The light

The light of God

God within

Praise God!

"Shout"

I yell because my words are mumbled
Free me my voice screams
Words scattered like pieces of a puzzle
I put them together
They sync in rhythm

With a black girls beat
Not skipping a beat
Mellow and deep
I let it flow
Together it rhymes

Without effort
These words are mines
Unbroken
Unique
They will stick

I put them together and let my voice be free
Released
I breathe
Free
Let it flow

My voice
My words
I shout it from the mountains for the world to hear
My voice so the world can hear
Stinging in their ears

My words will be my legacy.

"Psychic"

So 27 years later I am that little girl whose pain comes from the world in which she sées.
 A world she saw from her own lens in time and space throughout the decades.
 This little girl was psychic who saw the struggles before her time.
 That little girl, that teen, that woman is me.

CHAPTER 3

"Black Spaces"

"Black Holes"

I am Black

I was born sin and will die sin,

I have no value here on earth,

I am nothing mere of their equal,

There is no equation to my existence,

Suffrage, outrage and anger has become my story,

I see no hope and life has left my body on a new arising plane,

I am asleep and wish to remain awake from this nightmare,

I can foresee my future which ensures me no hope here,

I can remember my past which leads me here,

I am moving in and out of time,

My soul tormented eternally,

What will they read long after I am gone?

I am passing only a message in which time is drawing near to complete this,

I see a light of hope but a departure soon,

I am only a tiny beam of light passing through this incredible journey,

Time travel,

A journey through a different skin,

A different life after this life,

This journey I beg to differ the injustice and slaughter,

We are not our bodies,

Souls passing through a different dimension,

One I wish to exit,

One I wish no return,

What will be my next chapter after this?

Where will be my next light? Hopefully one of joy and peace.

I only fear here,

I do not fear the outer extensions of this body of life,

Who is God?

Am I God?

Will I not punish me for all that I've done and will do in this life?

I do exist here or there, past, present or future,

A billion trillion years in and out of space and time,

A universe awaits me,

I am a being moving through time,

And time is inevitable.

"Black Skins"

Black skins,

Black bodies,

Shed the dead epidermis layer peeling every layer of sin,

Bleeding hope seems not to cease our fears,

Raw uncut and not celebrated,

Ashamed, disgust, and hurt,

Aide our wounds as we bleed three degrees of separation,

Not their equal,

How long will we hurt?

From wounds that have scarred us up until this present day,

No ointment or bandage could ever cover our notorious history,

Our flesh not theirs, yearns to heal against the sun's ultraviolet rays,

Burn, burn, burn, till there is no feeling left,

We need to become numb in order to survive the brutality,

Flesh revealed we are still black,

Blood, we are still black,

Death we are still black on our head stones,

Black skins rotten leaving bones and old tales of pain,

Black bodies no more,

Ashes are left to the earth to consume for its production of life rebirth,

We rot without names,

Still yet, our Black lives give death our Black existence into the heavens,

Black lives give death our only true way of liberation,

Celebration,

Our black skins and bodies give us Black souls after we have been stripped from the living,

Souls either lost or tormented,

Some searching for the heavens,

Maybe a heaven for Black spirits that are burdened with pain for having Black skin,

Melanin

Just Black skins,

Unfree living with no riches,

Our soul must be freed,

"To Live"

It is here in this jungle that I become enraged,

Like a lioness without her cubs,

It is fear of the unknown oppression that awaits me now and, in the end,

A vicious cycle that seems to entangle my life,

I am nothing but matter,

I somehow exist in this God forsaken world,

It is me that becomes more and more like a beast as the days become darker, colder, unfamiliar,

I am lost somehow,

I yearn to be found,

How could this be a design from my wretched beginning till my end?

My unfortunate birth has led to a life of poverty and sadness and question of humanity

A love child,

Unwed,

Cursed,

Forgive my mother,

Forgive me,

Where is he?

The God that answers prayers,

Does he answer the Brown people of color or poor ones?

Somehow he has forsaken my breath,

I ask, why is it that we greet death with grief and sadness?

I celebrate their departing because somehow it is their humble beginning,

A new world apart from this hell on earth,

Tell me that heaven is not up in the clouds,

It is the soul outside this body,

I won't wait for Jesus to come and save me,

My skin is not white enough to enter the gates of heaven,

I am a sinner by birth,

I was never pure,

My skin is Black, Brown,

I won't argue with the church,

Outcast,

I am nobody,

God will never save me,

I pray so hard,

God!

Where is he?

The God that answers prayers,

Does he answer the Brown people of color or poor ones?

Somehow he has forsaken my breathe,

I ask, why is it that we greet death with grief and sadness?

I celebrate their departing because somehow it is their humble beginning,

A new world apart from this hell on earth,

Tell me that heaven is not up in the clouds,

It is the soul outside this body,

I won't wait for Jesus to come and save me,

My skin is not white enough to enter the gates of heaven,

I am a sinner by birth,

I was never pure,

My skin is Black, Brown,

I won't argue with the church,

Outcast,

I am nobody,

God will never save me,

I pray so hard,

God!

"Underscore"

I am nothing but a broke nigger

Broken dreams and hopes of tomorrow

Diminished and torn by society

I am nothing more than a mad black woman whose story is a question of suicide

My poverty has consumed my life

Pennies not dollars to get by if I try

My mirror can never be fixed

Never perfect

A broken mirror with an image whose eyes no longer aim for the prize

Who childhood expectations have been put on fire

No desire

Never perfect since birth

That cracked mirror stares a reflection of hopeless in despair

Why God has not saved me from this life of destruction

Wanting to escape this pain that has consumed my life

My body and mind not respected

Whatever nigger

Underscore

"Ring for Liberty"

I bleed these dying streets

I have no silver spoon or bronze in my mouth

Pennies, nickels and dimes jingles in my pocket

A black woman full of sorrow and grief

Serving a God that does not hear her pain

A woman who questions her place in the world

Life's misery

No joy here

Wipe your tears and comb your kinky hair

For hope is all I have and seek

It is the survival mode

The code of the streets, my community

Freedom has yet to ring the bell

A thousand Angels sing in her ears

The heavens have opened the gates

A world whose trouble is based on color, gender, and class

Crayola was never bright enough for me

Stagnant

The stars do not shine

The stripes do not wash every scar away

Lady liberty forfeited a dream

I could never be

Their world

Not mines

My wounds bleed more than a 400-year-old sin

How can I heal my scars?

They are so quick to drop labels

Stomped and sealed

I'm a slave to the game

I am nothing more than a primate, primetime drama and prime suspect

Mentally tormented

Distraught

Them and their profits

I am their product

Can I ever rise above their labels?

The lies I buy for a price to pay

Brainwashed and unconscious

I am awakened by the truth and light

They see us as bodies, numbers

Just research projects

Data, statistics

It's a sickening world without rights

Exclusive Black's and inclusive privileged America

Then I wonder why am I so depressed, mad and disturbed

My feelings and being consistently prosecuted and disregarded

Limited rights or perhaps none

Don't judge me from my words here

My reality is not distorted

I see my color

They see me

A reality designed for me

A reality not fiction

Truth be told

I need liberty!

"Skin"

Black skins
Black bodies
Bleed the dead epidermis layer
Peeling every layer of sin
Bleeding hope seems not to cease our fears
Raw and uncut and not celebrated
Ashame, disgust and hurt
Aide our wounds as we bleed 360 degrees of separation
Not their equal
How long will we hurt
From wounds that have scarred us until this present day
No ointment or band aid could ever cover our notorious history
Our flesh not theirs
Yearns to heal against the sun's Ultraviolet rays
Burn, burn, burn
Till there is no feeling left
We have become numb in order to survive the brutality
Flesh revealed we are still black
Death we are still black
Black skins
Rotten, leaving bones and old tales of pain
Black bodies no more
Ashes are left
Black
We rot
We are now one with earth
Still yet
Our black lives give death our black existence into the heavens
Our black skins and black bodies give us black souls after we have
been stripped from our flesh
Souls either contented or tormented
Some searching for the heavens
Some destined for hell!

"Case"

It's been so many trials and error that I should be running the courtroom,

I lifted my right hands so many times that at times I swear I am testifying in church, praising God or calling for answers,

I can't see truth when the room is full of lies and more lies,

How many times have I been tried and tested?

I've been tested so many that I became a law student,

I can't afford any fights,

It's a game you don't want to play,

Monopoly

The rich and powerful hone the show while the poor ones await their faith,

She's only guilty for being poor and also Black,

Where will her freedom lay?

Perhaps the blind dumb and deaf only hear his/her cries,

It only works for those who can afford to pay,

Not the ones in Urban America beat down in the concrete ghettos,

Those ghettos never had a chance from our birth,

Books with weight and confusion,

Whipped minds of the oppressed,

Under the hands of them and not God

Witch hunt and pinned crimes on innocent hands

Long wait, keep waiting, still waiting,

Where is Justina?

Blind folded with lies and they smile while we cry freedom.

"Labor"

I am the laborer who has given labor and has produced its goods,

Thirty six hours of pain and labor with no land in the land of the free

I am the producer of goods with none of my own to claim,

Just the clothes on my back and shoes on my feet,

I sweat to bleed, that has asunder the tears of my hungry belly that aches through the many nights of worry where will I rest my head,

Still, they dance in delight, sip tea, as their wealth has been consumed by my sacrifice,

I own nothing then my mind which no longer can be held by their deceitful modes of production,

The working poor in America, how hard do you work?

Poverty I know you we've been acquainted so long, that I feel you are a part of me,

Bourgeoisie: how do establish wealth and divide humanism?

Homeless where are you? There is land to claim,

Why three classes, why and who decides?

God where are you, or is it the Bourgeoisie that holds the 1% wealth of the world,

Why has it been that we were meant to suffer in a world of oxygen, trees, land and water,

Why can't we all be free?

Their design, power and corruption has held the power to decide my faith and decide my paths in this life

"Run Run Run"

Nigger run nigger run,
Nigger read nigger write
Your freedom
Fight
Read nigger read
Write nigger write

You ain't no slave
But a slave to the system
A rigged one for you
They can't stand for you to raise the bar
Know your rights
They can't stand for the slums to rise

They can't stand for you to raise the bar
Instead, they find ways to lock you behind bars
A system designed to cripple a race
Black skins bleed mercy
Whips and chains
Mental oppression

Modern times has found a way to dig in our backs
Free your mind nigger
They are coming for you
Run
Hide
Fight

Find liberation
They designed a whole new system
Mental freedom
Prism
Are we free?
Invisible chains dangle and jiggle

Liberate me
Liberate them

Our minds our bodies
Liberate us
Break our minds free
Liberate me!

"Riches"

My riches not in heaven and not here
Gold, Silver, Oil and diamonds
I have none
Stowaway
Runaway
Runaway from here

Liberate me
I want to be free
Material goods do not define me
Bells ring
Voices sing
The earth still

Where bodies lay low in dirt
And soil is rich but I'm poor
My back strong
My hands full
No riches for me
Heaven awaits me

Treasure and gold the pastor man says
I sing songs of praise waiting for the day
Earth is hell and heaven is sweet the church lady says
When everything around you freak you the fuck out,
I can't breathe my spirit leaves me every awakening day,
I can't stand the air I am forced to breathe every day,

I can't stand what my eyes are forced to see,
My spirit numb by the constant pain,
Who is my God and where is he?
I use to read about him in a book but these days I let it collect dust,
Ashes to ashes dust to dust,
Dead to me,

They say I'm blessed with a gift,

I am cursed by the gift,
I am suffering by his sacrifice to make my voice be heard,
I never choose to live in the ghetto,
I am fighting to keep my sanity,
Everyday it is a war that I can no longer plead to escape,

What is liberation?
Liberation is the soul,
Not here not up there but somewhere in time that cannot be found
in this life or timeline,
Cages,
Chains,
I yearn to break free,

Is this my life?
Hurt and disappointment,
What a wretch,
What a destined child to bare the struggle,
Where is my peace
Where is my joy?

Where is God?
Where are my riches?
I am cursed by his heirs,
I am cursed by my skin,
I am cursed by my ancestors sin,
I must wait for my liberation,

Joy cometh soon,
Peace cometh with sleep,
Riches will be in heaven they say
What about my riches today
My riches
My inheritance
Reparations pay

SLUMBER BODIES!

Slumber bodies grow restless by the day.
Their minds submit to their plans.
Liberties stripped away piece by piece.
The outspoken ones are considered fools and insane.
The world sleeps as they create a new order, a new world.
Shackle and chained, the cave is dark.
There is no light at the end and above their heads. Restless.
A new God, we've forgotten the old one.
The doors are chained.
The pews empty, the temple bare, the synagogues cold.
The people sleep, wake up, sleep, wake up.
Day after day.
The days go by and we wait.
We wait for a miracle.
We wait as they speak.
We wait for their assurance.
War is among this wretched earth.
A mental war.
An unseen war.
War we've never seen coming.
Justice, no justice.
Life, it depends on numbers.
It's dark and it gets darker by the day.
Where is light?
Where is liberty?
Where are the days we were free?
Have we ever been free?

"INJUSTICE DONE TO ME"

Can I tell you how many times the system tried to break me?
I remember when he raped me, I was just nineteen
Ripped my cherries and scared my body
I was called a possible jezebel just blackmail they didn't open a case

Dismissed by those to serve and protect
The shame and disgust, victim blaming
I hated myself
The kit stored for a joke

My panties
My panties again
DNA
Can't trust nobody she'd say

Take a bottle take a pull
Inhale and exhale and let the memories go
Let your coochie too because bitch you ain't special
You've been fucked over before

Can't you see they took without consent just smoke this and take the pain away
The pain rides deep into the back of your mind
Block and delete like a request you don't want to accept
You then ride in the back of some unknown car with flashing lights

That's the pain you felt bottled up inside turning into a mountain of rage
They throw you into a cage
You are ready to fight
Fight because that's all you had to defend yourself

Cop a deal and lose your rights
You fight

Long and hard without fist without weapons of war
They drag your name through the mud

You lose your ability to provide
You depend on a system that whips you to bend
You are now in a cycle of poverty and injustice
You eat but you are not full and worry

You sleep but your roof is not secure
You barely can wipe your ass
Little hands reach to you
They need you

You pray I will not be defeated
You pray to escape the system
You pray to beat your case
You pray to break free

Your memory drive uploads the injustice
Uploads the times you were a victim
then uploads the time you were the accused and charged
It uploads the pain and rage

It uploads be brave
Fight to buffer better times ahead
Fight to tell others I stand with you
Fight to use your voice and speak for those who cannot speak

Because injustice is something that can rip at your soul when
you are innocent
I know
Injustice
Injustice was done to me!

"Fighting"

Just break me from all of this
Emancipate this pain inside of me
Lord have you forsaken me now?
Why have all I known turned against me?

Lord, I pray this hurt inside will dissolve to hope and joy
Uplift me, hear my cry, Oh Lords of Lords
I just need to be free
The waters up against my neck

Fighting these waves of my life
Lord I can't give up this fight
Here I am all alone
Somehow I am trying to find this light

Darkness have succumbed to my life
Where sorrow and grief are all, I own
People wonder and they stare
How does this child survive it all?

My story, not all has been unfold
So many chapters that divide my life
If pain is what makes me write this poem
Why can't happiness sing me a song?

Lord I beg to differ from the realities of my life

Somehow I am accustomed for this fight of my life

Here in the tunnel searching away out

Trapped in a world that has forced me many times to hold my breath

Then I must at least try to breathe a sign of hope

Lord I still know you hold the keys but I beg to know the answers before I leave

The mountains seem so impossible at times

But I am still climbing without any destination

Lord I pray you heal my fears

Give me eyes to see the light so I could escape this darkness

The worst feeling to be trapped inside this gloomy cave

Searching and no way out

I've been through the storm

I've been through the heavy rains

I've been through every single hurt and pain

Lord I wonder if it's only me

Am I the only one in this world to think this way?

Lord, I'm asking am I still your child?

The waters have consumed me and I can't keep fighting these waves

I am now weak and need strength but I haven't received it in so long

Numb

Afraid

Did I lose my battle?

Courage can only save me from this war I fight

"Worn Out"

I am worn out like the soles of my shoe

I am worn out like the threads of my sleeve

I feel myself slipping away slowly and slowly

Holding onto the tiny bit of faith I have left

The days become more and more dreary

The nights become like cold shivers needing to find warmth

My cries leads to a river which man has yet to discover how deep it runs

A river that holds my sorrows and pain

A river that has drown my happiness

I no longer see the sunrise

I no longer howl at the moon, it does not appear in the night

How can I?

So much pain and grief

God where are you when I need you?

Have you abandoned your precious child?

You no longer comfort me

You don't even protect me from grief

Did you hear my cry last night when the world was still?

Did you hear my moans this morning?

How much shall I endure?

I am now feeling weak, no strength left

Hear me god, do you really exist?

Come on it's me your forsaking child

Have you turned against me?

You no longer care for me

Am I Lucifer's child?

Why am I tortured in my faith?

Why am I lost and afraid?

Between worlds

Whose child am I?

Sacrifice becomes the bitter truth

I will now lay my faith

Is it the light that bestows my faith?

It is the light that will restore my strength

But it will not shed the weight of pain

Mercy for me and all that I feel

The days aren't long because my days are soon,
There, I shall find him,
It's there I will confront him,
Curse him,

Ask him why he never saved me,
Ask why my sufferance,
Why me?
What a sadistic being,

I am forever a slave,
Where is freedom from all this?
I will never be free.
I am forever his child

"My Spirit Not Broken"

My God the heavens cry out for your people
We are fighting a good fight
With your mercy, grace and honor, the strength received,
We have been enslaved all this time,

Liberation exist through you
My Lord
We are merely mortal
We exist through you

Infinity and beyond
I fear not thy enemies who creep in the night
Darkness is in their eyes
Where light once exist

They seek my downfall
But I rise through you
My strength
My God

I am strong
My spirit not broken
I aspire to conquer the world
My gift my purpose my chosen destiny

What a fight
But I will make it
Shouting from the mountains
The world's greatest

Strength
Your light is upon me
Glory to God
Amen!

"FREE ME"

When everything around you freaks you the fuck out,
I can't breathe my spirit leaves me every awakening day,
I can't stand the air I am forced to breathe everyday,
I can't stand what my eyes are forced to see,

My spirit numb by the constant pain,
Who is my God and where is he?
I use to read about him in a book but these days I let it collect dust,
Ashes to ashes dust to dust,

Dead to me,
They say I'm blessed with a gift,
I am cursed by the gift,
I am suffering by his sacrifice to make my voice be heard,

I never choose to live in the ghetto,
I am fighting to keep my sanity,
Everyday it is a war that I can no longer plead to escape,
What is liberation?

Liberation is the soul,
Not here not up there but somewhere in time that cannot be found
in this life,
Cages,
Chains,

I yearn to break free,
Is this my life?
Hurt and disappointment,

What a wretch,

What a destined child to bare the struggle,
Where is my peace?
Where is my joy?
Where is God?

Where is my riches?
I am cursed by this air,
I am cursed by my skin,
I am cursed by my ancestors sin,

I must wait for my liberation,
Joy cometh soon,
Peace cometh with sleep,
The days aren't long because my days are soon,

There, I shall find him,
It's there I will confront him,
Curse him,
Ask him why he never saved me,

Ask why my sufferance,
Why me?
What a sadistic being,
I am forever a slave,

Where is freedom from all this?
I will never be free,
Please show me,
I must make a way.

"NIGHT"

You ever felt the pit of your womb in which everything turns
The solace of the night is the only peace and comfort in which you
are all alone
The cries of the weak and misfortune
You can't help to think
I ask God but no reply

The lies I am constantly fed by a society who mocks me
Beast roam and herds try and flee the wrath of destruction
Created
I won't tell you I am a victim
The creation of power

I am within this dark cave bounded and chained
I see the light unable to move
Unable to speak
Unable to reach the light above me
I yearn to break free mentally

What is free?
I am physically free they say
The powers infringed on a society with disparities
Am I insane?
Built like walls to silence my voice

I do not sleep during the solace of nights
Is it my soul and mind moving before time?
Time is a moving thing
A thing beyond the Galaxy a trillion light years away
My body does not move against the clock that ticks away

My mind however chases the sun away
It has seen many days and days before this
Travel
Time
Solace night the stars shine!

"The New Rising of Order"

Kinky head child with skin so dark where is your father,

The one who made you to sin infinite the one you call your God,

You jump up, lift your hands and sing so loud and shout,

Still he hasn't come to save you from the wreckage that has cursed you and those before you,

Isn't it enough the poverty that has consumed you?

Oh that promise land is a comfort to a fool,

How long will your people wait for him over 400 years and still no savior,

The destruction that has consumed your villages, stolen your babies, and destroyed your men,

High tides at noonday while the war continues to manifest causing more self-destruction than the old whips and chains,

All those toys held in the very palms of your hands has blinded you from the truth,

Distracted near blind as you have given up your liberty that you fought to earn and was never rewarded,

My property, not God's in a world where power is needed for order,

The day will come when you won't even breathe paper or see the words that your ancestors fought to read,

Now your children will no longer be in need to learn, we'll dispose of intellects for our own intellectual property,

We your oppressors have dominated and control you ever going, this will not end as has been in the beginning,

Those like you sing songs of hope, you write words of hope and speak words of hope, still yet the your battle is ever going,

Civil never guarantor your rights to complete freedom,

I may have took the chains physically, but the mental is more destructive to your people,

You can't be free if I attack your mind, there is no liberty and you will never be liberated,

Your mind is an extension of your body it is more precious than the skins that have bled in hopes of freedom,

Your mind is more precious to me and I will consume its every purpose,

Perhaps deeply there's a soul that exist besides what we see but we can destroy it once we have conquered their minds,

Go ahead and pursue liberation, but the frustration of your ghetto designed by me will only keep you in despair losing hope,

We cannot afford you to conquer our plans,

We must cease all intellects that seek to overcome our plans,

We know the war will eventually reverse and conquer us, the oppressors and destroy our class order,

But first we must attack those with the greatest potentials in the world, so that they may not rise up against us,

But even we cannot guarantee that all will remain in order as a new order seeks to take over the old order,

"My Hope For Tomorrow"

It is easy to claim the silver and bronze boots in a fairy tale and in a book.

I wish I could but the truth is I was nowhere near at birth and I'm nowhere close right now.

The only thing is hope, even as tiny as a mustard seed.

Somehow I believe that my oppressors will eventually free us.

Somehow that's a fairytale I wish to keep.

I must believe.

Although we are physically free it is the mental games they play that keep us in chains.

Yearning to be free from this cave.

I see the light above the darkness but it seems it's only me who is aware that I must truly escape from all the madness.

Led to believe there is no other way but to remain in chains.

Their words fed into the minds of those who are generational curses carrying the same chains as our ancestors dreamed we would be free, break these chains.

Mental torment is worse than the physical whips that bled the skins of slaves.

I just want to break free, no oppression, just liberation.

Free I say like MLK.

I got to break free.

Why has oppression led to my depression?

Feeling hopeless at times like this is the end.

What kind of God do I serve that was given to us with whips and chains, allowing torment and pain.

Why?

Why color?

Why racism, classism, and all this damn division?.

I don't want to live thinking that bondage is all it will ever be and that I will and can't be free.

Ashamed of my class, the bottomless pit, ashamed not because of my color but how it's ten times harder to escape the burden that will possibly await my future generation like me and those before me.

I must release these chains of bondage.

I see the light.

I hope for liberation and no longer do I want to remain oppressed.

I hope to break free.

I hope to escape this trap that has been designed from my birth canal the moment I enter.

I am not my skin.

I am a human being whose soul is free and more far superb than what you see.

Hear my mind speak, it speaks through my soul is who I am.

My soul is free and beyond this world.

I am my soul, my soul of hope and freedom.

My hope for tomorrow.

Hoping tomorrow my soul will be free.

"Royal"

I am not your pet project
I am not your slave
Bondage and chains
Break these chains
My people will not be fooled

You've had your time
And we will come to take back our thrones
Our Kings and Queens
We have been given orders from a higher being a higher God
whose anger and fury reigns from the heavens

My people will not submit to your plans
You've built walls to contain our minds
We are no longer in prison
Break these fucking bars now

You've created ghettos and slums
Having my people fooled there is no escape
Liberation is ours
Freedom rings

We will take back our wealth
Rubies and diamonds
Pearls deep in the sea
Holding treasures of power

We've held it all this time
We've held your children down
Suckling our milk
We want our cows and pastures

Royalty in our blood
Our DNA is not for sale
A flow of riches through our veins
We want our data

Fuck what you thought
We built your ships
We have sacrificed our own
This world is ours

Our gold, silver and bronze
Our oil
Our minerals and metals
Rich in soil

We are the kings and queens of this earth
We are taking back what's ours
We are not your pet project
We are not your data

We are humans with souls who must be liberated!

Black Spaces

My PTSD won't let go of my black spaces

Spaces in between my life of 45

This ain't about you and you and how you feel

This is about that little black girl who was called a nigger by the pool

This is for that teen girl who was mocked and ridiculed, and kit exploited her DNA she never saw justice

This is about that woman whose been hustled by the system, beaten and broken, oppressed by their system, she had no silver spoon or bronze on her plate

This is for that mother who witnessed police brutality and corruption against her daughter who was then thrown through revolving doors of the Justice system

A system that dictates with hate against our beautiful black and brown children

A system converting them to unknown beast that's PTSD

This is for that black educated sister who is fighting to find her place in society that undermines her ability and pays her under the belt, the wage gap

She's constantly counting nickel and dimes and pays the price because her loans is still waiting

Forgive her forbearance

This is for that beautiful brown skin girl whose dolls under and over represent true beauty within

This is for the many spaces in between black lives causing PTSD

You just don't forget the trauma

I didn't forget

Forget how I felt like the nigger you called me at thirteen

Forget how he got away with a piece of me, my innocent me, my cherry

Forget how every time I was a dollar short and bills late the hurdles, I jumped to keep the roof over our heads

Forget how my black spaces left black circles and marks from what I thought was love because I really needed my father to show me love

Forget how I witnessed my daughter's trauma with fear and rage that the hate was real and sent her through the doors of hell for more than a year till she was weary and weak

Forget how I see black and brown people in my community who can't seem to escape the poverty, through eras of trauma living with PTSD

Forget how I realized the bottles, the joints and crack pipes were just an escape from trauma

That the pills ain't enough to erase these black spaces

These black spaces holding deep trauma

Deep wounds

Deep scars

These black spaces in our minds are so deep that we create a space in time to find a way to heal

CHAPTER 4

Her Dying Love and Sex Died With Him."

"Verse"

Sweet like honey running between my toes
Sweet like sugar the melody humming off my tongue
Sweet like brown sugar dipped in my tea

I sip
We dip
Ummm, just right

Inhale
Exhale
The taste lingers buzzing on the tip of my tongue

The smell intoxicates me
It lingers like parfum
Sweet

I get high
Without a doubt
I can't help but to love it

I embrace myself for it gets stronger
I'm addicted
It becomes my drug of choice

I'm strapped letting the rush excite me
A euphoria takes hold of me
I fight the urge but I give in

This high I cannot lie
It's like heaven on earth
I hear the angel sing

Sing!

I sing along

Then you join in

We sing with joy

Sweat

Sweet

Salty

The pitch becomes higher

Then a pause

I go soprano

You alto 2

The chorus becomes silent after the last note

I am stuck in a trance

Eyes are locked

We take a final breath

Heavy

Inhale and exhale

Repeat

Searching Self

"Mr. Lover"

He almost took a piece of me, almost forever gone and never to reclaim

Yeah my lover, my ex I should say

My spirit, my soul, my mind

Even my delicate vagina was at stake

Yeah he took it almost

Nearly four years to reclaim it back

All the mess he dragged into my life

He's been Facebooking, Instagram, Whats App and texting me

My number one follower it seems

Liking all my pictures and statuses

Almost or is he obsessed with me

It was all physical when we were together and I mean physical by all means

Now this shit is mental, technical abuse I see

Poking my every move

Shit am I gullible not to unfriend him after everything we've been through, this scum bag

I thought I loved him endlessly

I thought I needed him infinity

I thought I missed him but it's an obsession

Or perhaps my self-esteem he had destroyed before

I became his possession once his property

Finally I was wanted and someone loved me I thought

It was so good

So good sexually, so good mmm, ooh, ahh so good,

He made me feel real good, real, real, good,

Other times he made me feel weak, hopeless and dead

The beatings and fights

Threat for my safety

I saw death in his eyes, I felt fear in mines,

I saw him killing me spiritually slowly and surely, mentally and emotionally, just killing me, killing me harshly inside,

Nearly four years to reclaim it all to go back in that same deep dark hole

I can't, will not, won't go back to toxic shit

Why am I losing myself in all this?

You wanted all of me

You leave me no choice I need all of my things

I need my spirit back

I need my mind back

I need my vagina back

I need it all back

I want back me the one you stole

You took me away

I didn't mean for it to end this way

I just thought we, you and I could work things out in my mind at least

Seems like nothing changed

You are still the same boy who preferences of toys arewomen like me

Women who allow men like you to kill them inside

Sex is down the drain it use to be sweet, so hot, so sticky, so wet between my thighs

Excitement no longer resides between us

The well is now dry

And I can't even thirst anymore

I have to redeem myself from all this pain

I ask myself, why did I let you in my domain?

Why not another host?

Desperate for a man who can't and will never love me

A man who acts like a boy and treat women like toys

I am so over the games you played

I was so blind I could not see there was no love and I had no self-love

Imprisoned by it all scarred for life

How can I ever trust again?

Removing brick walls, concrete, metal, glass chains

Locked away so stay away

Never to be revealed again by you

My love will never be free, never be free with you again

It took too long to regain my self worth and I won't let you rip it apart

My heart is not yours to destroy

Mr. Lover more like the devil

You tricked me with your sweet lies and games you played

"My Ex"

My ex that sex I can't forget

It was raw and uncut

The shit that Pornhub would love

Fans only

Your only fan

Shit had to cool down between us

There were times it was hot and heavy

Heavy hands make bangs sunglasses with a touch of covergirl

Fashionista looking like Mona Lisa on any given day

Covered in veil to hide the scars imperfections you caused me

I had to cover your lies and cheats in between the sheets

You made me feel real good real good and then somehow I'm afraid and sad

Your words were nothing more of sheer lies of deceit

You just wanted chocha and my chocha could have gotten sick but thank God she and me is covered

Covered by a veil unknown

You sick mother fucker

I once use to feel for you but now the feelings are faded but the memories of hurt live

You sent a message I could not reply

There was that same old rage from that boy I once knew who sounds like you

I read it with concern and said "oh hell no" I am not the same girl
she's Queen

She ain't looking for validation

She earned her crown

She ain't looking for comfort

She is royalty

You can't be on that same level

She upgraded mentally physically and spiritually you just can't
understand

She has standards and has been through it all

That woman you knew is now a Queen who has a crown

You are not the King she desires at the throne to be

You were not the one and surely not now

Sayonara, Au Revoir, Adios, Good bye

You are not the guy for me

You were never the guy for this Queen

We are not the same

Your just a faded evanesce memory

CHAPTER 5

"Conversation With God"

"Steps"

Just trying to stand upon ground
These days my knees are weak
I do not eat

My body has transition to ports unknown
My mind has calculated steps not seconds
Time moves like a beam of light

My eyes have seen the glory
My God
You are worthy to be praised

Believers with faith, hope in despair
We still call your name
Life, amazing grace

How bittersweet
I do believe
Because I've been saved many times

Behold the beauty
The blind cannot see
My eyes have seen the glory

My faith
I somehow still believe
You are my God!

"Here For The Show"

I "saw a page in my journal April 4th 2021
The physical pain and torture my body fought for its spiritual and mental aguish
All my life i have been tortured as a creative soul
And here I have decided to fight with all my might
I only fought for the show
Even Though I found pleasure and pain in my body crossing
I saw light through a dark tunnel
Several breaths in and out
Belly flat I prayed
Alone at night besides the stars
I cried out
For once he comforted me
Like a child I swept
Not knowing if I was gonna live or die
Like so many I knew
I didn't get to live my purpose
Pen and paper
To the eyes of many
Through the ears of many they hear my voice
To the wind
To the Hills and Mountains
I will speak
Because he saved me that my voice may speak and my pen may write
I am here to tell my story untold
Alive and well I am here for the show

"God"

My God the heavens cry out for your people
We are fighting a good fight
With your mercy, grace and honor, and the strength received,
We have been enslaved and free all this time

Liberation exist through you
My Lord
We are merely mortal
We exist through you

Infinity and beyond
I fear not thy enemies who creep in the night
Darkness is in their eyes
Where light once exist

They seek my downfall
But I rise through you
My strength
My God

I am strong
My spirit not broken
I aspire to conquer the world
My gift my purpose my chosen destiny

What a fight
But I will make it
Shouting from the mountains
The world's greatest

Strength
Your light is upon me
Glory to God
Amen!

PRAISE!

Praise him from my soul I feel him
Praise him from my heart within
Praise him for he I rest with comfort
Praise him for his divine protection

Praise him for providing for me
Praise him for he is my fortress
Praise him for his mercy for me
Praise him for he is my strength when I am weak

Praise him for he watches over me
Praise him for he is my friend in this lonely world
Praise him for he has never turned his back away from me
Praise him for he keeps me in his hands like a new born baby

Praise him for he has made my enemies my footrest
Praise him for he has crowned my head and washed my feet with
his blessings and mercy
Praise him for I am his and he is my Lord my King
Praise him! Praise him! Praise him!

"Light"

It is the darkest days you struggle to find light
Alone in the night my heart beats to find joy in the morning
All my days have been weary
My soul aches to find peace

Torment and judgment is all I ever known
You said you are a judge of judges
You are the God of God's
The majestic one

It's you I lift my hands
Weak and feeble
I have begged to be humble
This life I live is what I've known

Headache and pain
I grieve throughout my days
I struggle to find strength even as tiny as a mustard seed
Faith

As tiny as a mustard seed
Alone in the night
I pray to you but you keep silent
I cry

Where are you to comfort me?
Your Queen
The moon promised me
The stars shine brightly

I saw your beauty
The eyes do not lie
My God My King
Protect me

Keep me in all your grace
Mercy

My tears have cried a river
A trillion miles of sea

I embrace your blessings even when I can't see
Please cover me
My feet are weak
The sea

The sun
The light
I love to see your glory
My God

I cry with heavy heart
My soul begs for peace
Your will is your mercy
Cover my soul

The Alpha and the Omega
It was written
The creation and destruction
The good and the bad

The light and dark
You are my author
I am your writer
Published in your grace

"Tree of Life"

Damn, I shed tears again like every fucking year.
Good grief I wear black, my dark days when the good go young
But still fucking here and I don't deserve to be here because there
is no innocence.
I asked for forgiveness and haven't realized your mercy and grace
that has brought me thus far
I am a worthless ungrateful bastard your child
I haven't heeded your word and have disobeyed your honor

Still you open my eyes each day
Pain and sorrow would consume my days but you somehow
rescued me
I have seen the world it's heavy to bare
My chest
My heart
My mind

With every blood that runs through my veins eternal life awaits
me
Lifting your name
You have taken pure gold and turned them into wings like angels
I've lost but gained so many by my side
Cover them oh God that they may watch over us
Your precious angels

You choose the plan
No questions
We plan you take
You are God
I cried to die but you kept me
I know it's your will it's ill

You forgave me my Lord my savior
Who saved a wretch like me
Please shed light on me
Let that light shine bright as the star

Despite the pain and grief I feel at times
I know my words and voice is a testimony and hope for the weak

Please, these days fade
The people I love fade
And the tree withers away
The leaves fall
And the stems crack with each passing year
Heal my roots so that I can grow in your spirit

Forgive us lord
Nurture us with your spirit
Fill us with your word
Fill us with your grace and mercy
Anoint us with your divine protection and keep us safe
Give me strength to carry this load despite at times its too much to
bear, chosen

"SEEDS"

My tears gliding like a rivers stream
My crown blessed with his glory and clemency
My feet blessed by his compassion
I've seen my years unfold before me like a story waiting to be told
I see my life being told to the unheard
My words unfolding uttering from my lips I speak

Bless thee
Not curse thee
Forgive the world that live or dies
The universe within this body
Journey
Scars

Heal
This life whose breathe breaths life inside of me
Here I stand at your leniency
Mercy
I have been caught by your divine exalt
My years of tribulations

Was I born to labor
All my life I have given fight
Charged battles and front lines
My eyes only leads rivers unknown
I have witnessed my seed defy me
Curse me

Hate me
Tell me these are lies
Has the woes of the world taken her precious spirit
The bright sun illuminated a child in merriment and love
The joys and wonders of life are now dreadful and sunless
Weary and cold

The weight of the world
Pain
Innocent minds lost
Where is the light?
Like most, give them the light and enlighten their minds to find
that lost child inside
My tears gliding like a river

Ripples at my feet
Tugs at my heart
I was once that girl enraged at the world
I was afraid
I pray
My seed stay in the light

The rain nourishes
The sun will guide you
I have faith
Believe
My seed
Seasons change and harvest will come someday

The rivers have cried enough for me
Cleansed my feet
Washed my eyes and face
I pray that you too one day will see with your eyes
I pray that you too will feel the glory and praise
I pray my crown inspire your own honor and story

My seed, I pray!

"IMAGINE JOY"

There are days when my spirit feels as it has left my soul and I am numb to people places and things

Imagine getting up every day questioning when will the war begin and how will it end

I pray each day no war

Imagine bearing it all to yourself because the ones you have are already spiritually broken and weak and fighting their own war

Imagine who's left has either their soul snatched or their spirit unrepairable

Imagine all avenues and doors have been closed and you are left without any solutions and assistance

Imagine feeling the unbearable pain sharpen in your chest and you are left holding your breath not knowing when the time comes

Imagine all the years you fought to live for them and now you are fighting these days to live and you pray for God to take you home because you do not want to commit the first act of sin

Just imagine keeping it all bottled up inside

Imagine your world closing in on you

Imagine the joy you brought into the world becoming nothing more than an hallow dark of nothing who wishes daily to snuff your lights out

Imagine living with negativity and it curses you and steals any chance you may have of joy replaced with anger and rage

Imagine you giving up to make a home worth living to now being excited to sleep anywhere even the concrete streets because home is not a home

It's a home of chaos and misery

Violence and destruction

Imagine you express your concerns to the doctors and the system but they just turn a blind eye

They send them home with instructions that means nothing because they can't comply

They can't comply because the mind has faded into chaos and confusion

Emptiness

Just imagine your voice being unheard and you are left constantly picking up the pieces

Glasses everywhere

Broken pieces you wonder if you'll ever put them back together

Imagine your days going empty but full of fear

Fear that all you hoped and dreamed of becoming is a nightmare

Imagine seeing your seed being torn and rooted in something you never planted

Nowhere to turn

You are left alone trying to find peace and solace but the tides are never ending

Despite you holding on

Just imagine life continuously throwing Murphy's law and you are fighting it all without weapons

Without grenades

Without help

Without answers

You are just riding the waves hoping to be saved

Despite feeling weary

Despite your drowning faith

And the pain growing by the day

You pray that God will somehow save you

Save you from your troubles

Lift you up and take you away

Away to a place long promised long awaited

Home as they say

Home

Because you know there is final

Life is only short of the promise

The promise land the heaven the afterlife where joy cometh in the morning

Final

Joy

That's all you wanted in this life and nothing or anything ever fulfilled that need

You yearned all your life

But life only came with sorrow and grief

Disappointments and anger

Setbacks and challenges

You become weak cursing and questioning God

Why?

Where is my joy?

Can you heal my pain?

God when will be the day?

Where is joy?

"UNTITLED"

I have seen the light
It reigns from the sky

So high
Praise be to God

The earth shook
My feet weak by his grace

Infinity is his grace
Your majesty

My Lord
There is none above you

My eyes have seen your light
I am blessed by your love

You choose me
Your child

Your words comforts me
Your love surrounds me

Your spirit protects me
You are God!

CHAPTER 6

Steps to God, Steps to Her Crown, She is a Queen"

"Grown"

I slip my dress careful not to pull to hard over my Fenty
The cap manages to stay in place not another virtual insult to
maintaining my hair
Black girl shit
Hours to get fly

Each braid holding what little youth is left
Botox without Botox
It's how we tighten our skin
The pain is the sacrifice for beauty

My momma always said "hold your head in place"
Those days a comb would fly if not still
So you did your best to bear the pain
I'm grown and still bear the pain

My pain to maintain my youth
My pain to smile despite how I feel inside
I'm too grown to cry
Mascara and all don't run from the truth

Highlight my cheeks the ones that was once full
My youth has betrayed my beauty
Years of deceit
I realized that I once had that light

Highlight what once was there
I brush twice along my forehead just in case a line or two wants to
bare my age

I am now faced with insecurities that I am getting old
I know I am grown

I have grown to acknowledge that age comes with a line or two
A Strawn of grey soon becoming a head full too
Where is the fountain of youth?
For my bones that ache

And knees that beg mercy
The pain of being grown
No pill prescribed for grown
Just memories of my youth

I wish not to be grown
But I am grown with grown women shit
Grown not to crack, wrinkle or dimple in my thighs
Grown and gray protruding through the dye

I am grown enough to know the lines
The lines that remind me of my youth
I straighten the lines and hope for it fades away
Grab my brush and highlight the high

Grown with years and decades
Grown to know shades of gray
Grown to know time is beyond my wrist
I look in the mirror with that little girl looking back at me

"MY SHOES"

I am not woman

I am woman with many shoes for every problem there's a new shoe to tell a story Looking at my life I'm getting ready strap these laces and strap them tight

I'm getting ready to walk out those doors and start my life like a brand new shoe fresh out the box

I need a new beginning

I am that woman

I am that woman who's willing to transform into a queen

I understand that Queens have problem before they inherit their throne through all the mud and dirt, sweat and tears

I am that woman

I am that Queen

I deserve my throne

I am that woman

I am that queen

I am the goddess the creator it is me it is me that carries my offspring to inherit the throne

I am not woman

I am a Queen and like I said I got a pair of shoes for every chapter in my life with a story

I have walked a trillion miles unknown

I had to journey long to get here

They see the patterns they see the prints they see the colors but they can't see my inside

They can't see my story within they can't see my struggles they
only see my success to the throne
They only see me rise but I've always kept my eyes on the prize
I am that woman I am that Queen
I will fight for my throne I will fight for my inheritance
I am that woman I am that woman

I am that woman that will never give up
I am that woman that will always fight
I am that woman that Queen that goddess with inside me there's
a God that rages a God that fills me up with strength and honor
integrity and dignity
I will inherit my throne
I fought and never gave up because that's what Queens do

"Women Like Me"

There are girls like me

Women like me

Fighting bullies throughout school

Fighting the courts and system that has kept us trapped

Fighting constant barriers that make us feel like throwing in the towel

There are women like me all over this world and especially right here in America

We are a dime away from homelessness and a dollar short to survive

We are fighting wage gaps

We are always fighting that loan officer

We are fighting stigmas designed to tear our self confidence

Corporate America is not ready for us

We are sitting in the back and not at the head of that table

There are women like me that could be CEOs and SEOs but we are sweeping and mopping your floors

Changing your babies diapers

Mothering your children

Giving care to your mother's

We are constantly on our knees pleading with God

We are fighting to survive

Land of the free

There are women like me singing songs of hope

There are women like me

Scholars but poverty is their stricken grief because their underestimated by their skin,yet it bleeds

There are women like me who just want the opportunity to rise
and be free
Make their voices heard
Women who want to be liberated
Who want to be acknowledge by society
There are women like me
Women like me who yearn to tell their story
Women like me whose voices needs to be heard

Queen

Awwwww. I scream loud
I am angry so I frown
Queens like me are warriors, constantly fighting wars like
warriors
We are on the front lines like soldiers
We are the head of the fish but society treats us like tails
We are the breadwinners, we champion up strength
We aren't seen weak like our ancestors who have held many
plantations down
She had to sacrifice
Underground she would die to let her children be free
My black sisters know about sacrifice
Her child is who her life and soul is
Look at our ghettos
The life of a single black mother holds more weight
She must muster up courage and strength to bare it all
There is no king to support her rib, that is a lot of weight to hold
But they say we are mad
We just had to adapt alpha
Alpha made us forget our feminism
We never needed a man or better yet we never had men to hold us
up
We have been raped our goddess
Let us not forget we are goddesses
We rule
Stand tall

Lift my head to the sky
I am that black woman
Not mad
A warrior a Queen

"Goddess"

I am a woman because they call me woman

I am a goddess because I possess the attributes of a woman and powers like a God

I am the daughter who came from a mother who is a woman

And I am a woman who became a mother like my mother

I am the estrogen that has soiled the sheets after two spirits collide

Still I keep my composure as a lady when I walk these streets or ride, as I am expected to do so by Mr. Society

Whose expectations of dilemma, stigma and stereotypes tries defeats my purpose

Somehow you expect me to swallow shit and keep quiet

Because Mr. Society says so

Fuck you and you and you all

Oops that's not for a lady to say

I won't apologize for smoking my cigarette as I grab a bottle of this whiskey and smoke my weed

Inhale and exhale long puffs and deep thoughts

Not typical don't be critical

No red wine, red pumps, red dress, red painted nails and lips

Waiting for another fucker, screw up poor old ass sucker

I won't wait, anticipate, excite as you pull up

Testosterone

Musk

Muscles

Go fuck off

I'm not that type of lady

I got this man

Hand this over

One, two, three, four nails cornered

Drill, screws, and hammer

No I won't beat a bitch but I will you if you challenge me

I'm gonna fix this my nigga

This door right here is mine and I own it

An extra lock and keys but not for you

Let's see if you can enter don't bother to try

I couldn't wait patiently for you to decide

We got this over here

I am woman now hear me roar and to let you know this is my jungle

Single mother all alone and I am colored

I am not a mammy, jezebel or welfare queen

No daddy here, just me, just like my mother

Tight ship

I'm captain and I pay the price to make my home alright

I am a bread winner, hustler, just like my fellow brother

No sympathy here my dear

No Kleenex needed

No tears here

Cause I'm not broken

I won't whimper like Scarlet O' Harrah

Panting and waiting for him to cruise my ship or wreck my ship

I got God within me

Because I am a God who is a woman

Therefore I got this man

I'm just as good, even better than a man

My mother contributed and we never suffered

So why do the two heads of household shit?

Fables and make believe stories in society

I didn't need him and she didn't either

I didn't grow up smelling musk in the living room after supper

It was our world where as women run shit

Else babies would cry endlessly, endlessly

Mouths unfed, clothes worn out, shelters without tops

All that she bred was labor

Long hours, short pay, bills paid, legs closed, chipped nails, stale hair, worn jeans, head of household

Was and is a woman in our world

Who is a Goddess?

A god

A woman

Not a dominant man who claims to be a god's gift to us

Dreaming football, outing flames, laying bricks, hard hats, rusty boots, long beards

Dirty jeans, rusty nails

Pooping beer tops after a long day and grabbing their crotch

Just like my brother

I beg to differ from that Barbie world shit where we are constantly questioned and undermined

I am the labor and giver of the world

Without us this world would never exist

We give life or we can destroy it before it has a chance

So without us men wouldn't exist

Earth is our delivery

I am a god who is a woman

I am the production of a man's labor, my labor, a woman's labor

Who gives delivery in a world that questions us?

This is our world and we run it.

"Goddess Too"

I am a God my eyes see the glory and darkness of this world,
My pain and grief heart broken, shattered hopes and dreams for
my youth
The chains beneath earth's feet
I have borne the seed of many offsprings
Many nations
My tears the seven seas across the world that calls my name

I am light in their eyes
I am the voice that lifts a nation
I am the beat of the drums
They dance to my name
They chant for me, their tongues utter my name
My presence before them makes them bow before me

Centered on stage
I am that light in their eyes
I am that voice of hope
My words do not fade they penetrate minds
I am their leader
These are my people

Hear my voice
I am the voice of the unheard
My eyes have seen it's glory
I am a God a goddess, my children
This earth has been our fortress
I have given birth to a nation

The heavens have blessed our vaginas
Our vaginas brings life
Our universe within breathing life into beings who flood the earth
since birth
Our milk nurturing babies sweet from our bosoms we sweep for
their souls
Our bodies our vessels our blood running through their veins
We Gods Goddesses where life begins within

Goddess of fertility bear fruits of our labor
Goddess of justice fight for our sins
Goddess of the moon give us light in the dark
Goddess of the sun may you brighten our days
Goddess of water quench our dying thirst
Goddess of storms may you clear a path for us

"Women Are Gods"

Women are Gods so bestow your respect and honor upon us,

Women have created generations who will one day rule this nation,

Women have harvested the seeds implanted, we shall nurture our offsprings and give life new meaning,

Women are the earth's soil there is no life without us,

We want to be the God of love,

The God of forgiveness,

The God of Rebirth and transformation,

We want to be the God of legends

The God of truth,

The God of all humans,

But somehow we are the God of pain before joy if any,

Let us nurture their minds and hearts and influence their ways,

She will rise when the sun is dark and the days become night,

She shall overflow a river when thirst is upon her,

She provide because somehow she survive,

She survive and she will rise,

Destiny and time can only be defined,

Traveled far from a star a billion light years,

She is not afraid nor will she fear the coming days of an evolutionary wrath from war,

For her mind will be of courage and truth,

For the God of gods lives within her,

Her body just a vessel carrying spirit a from the omnibenevolent,

God is within her, therefore, she is a god a Goddess.

"DEAR QUEEN"

Dear queen you've endured so many seasons and chapters of your life

You always believed thats why your still here

Just trust and believe that better days are ahead where little girls dream rainbows and the rain clears

Let your light shine again and light that fire inside

Open that chapter and begin

Write your story and change that character

Create the life you desire

Pen and paper manifest and believe because dreams do come true

We have the power to create our destiny that we always desired within your heart and mind

Poverty is not mines nor yours to claim

Happiness is yours and mines to claim

Trials and errors is our testimony

From rags to riches we dream we live

Every little girl desires her castle, dream

Take the throne and take your crown queen

Rise rise rise up

The world has been waiting on you

Stand tall

Your crown and glory

They shout "Hail to the Queen"

"CROWN HER YOUR GLORY"

Crown her with all your glory
Crown her with all your mercy
Crown her with all your grace
Crown her with all your blessings
Crown her with the light

Bestow the light upon her crown
Bestow upon her the insight and knowledge
Bestow your love and protection
Bestow your divine powers within her
Bestow upon her your majesty, your blessings

Cover her
Protect her
Hold her
Love her Lord
Forgive her sins

Create a new spirit within her
Let her candle light the minds of the forgotten
Give her the gifts to share with those who have forgotten theirs
Ignite passion in her to speak the words of the broken and heal
the wounds of the sick
Give her the courage and strength to help those who have given
up to rise up again

Crown her with the words of wisdom
Crown her with the knowledge to see the ways of the world

Crown her with all your mighty strength

Crown her with royalties long awaited to give the world

Crown her with the stars aligned in her purpose

Little girl speak up the Queen is here

Little girl this is your day

Little girl you are now the voice that now speaks

Little girl shine that light bright

Never stop dreaming because the universe awaits your testimonies

Queen you have earned your crown

Queen you have fought battles untold unseen

Queen you have fallen and risen higher than any eagle in the sky

Queen you have endured seasons for various reasons

Queen you are favored and blessed please rise

"Crown"

I lost the old her and this new woman here I do not know

She's different she's beautiful with all her scars and all she has been through

She somehow manages to keep light despite all the darkness she's seen

She somehow managed to keep a dream hidden in her pocket tiny as faith

She managed to believe, believe that somehow her rainy days will bring rainbows

She never lost faith in all her days despite her songs full of pain

She just kept the faith and believed that someday she would rise

Rise higher than any object in the sky to achieve her dream

Rise higher than any rags to riches story ever told to her

Rise higher than any sun seen hitting the core of the earth from her eyes

Rise higher than any moon and stars that has given her light

Rise higher than their expectations and odds that have been stacked against her

Rise higher than anything, dream, vision she had imagine

Rise higher than the flames burning for her who kept her desires and dreams alive through the fire

That little girl staring at me still has a light

She points me to the new woman

The one with all the scars and stories of pain

She smiles and stares at me

She whispers I am not broken

She's beautiful

She's a God

She's a Queen

She stands tall

With dignity and grace

That woman that woman that woman is me

The one I dreamed

Rebirth

The old woman is gone and this Queen is me

"King"

I believe my king is coming for me

I believe he's there to save me

I hear they chant his name across the seven seas

I hear his light it shines brightly

I've been waiting for him to save me

By the waters I'm deep for his love

Please my king don't let me drown come save me

Heal this heart

Set me on the mountain facing the sun

Set me up on the hills and let them see your Queen

Let them chant my name as they chant yours from afar across the seven seas

My king will you help me

I've been waiting since I was a little girl

I tried not to believe in fairytales, folklore and make believes

But I somehow believe that you will come even if I'm old and gray

I hope because my heart is still young not broken beyond repair

A new sun

A new day

A new chapter

A new page

"Trees"

Its leaves fall for me

Its branches I see

It's sacrifice made for me

Tall and firm

Leaf by leaf

For paper

My book

What a sacrifice it bares for me

Bless this tree blesses this tree for me

With glee and honor

This tree you see is here before your eyes

Who's words hard like stone

Forever

Tree

It was sacrificed for me to write these words on paper

"FIRE"

Set my soul on fire

Burning for these words I shout

Set my soul on fire may it light the dark where I once was afraid

My soul here to speak

This thing inside me gives me eyes to see

Hands to write

In the night skies the world is my window

The feather floats through air

Can you feel my words?

Can you hear my voice?

From the hills I've cried

From the mountain I climbed

I trembled and fell at times but I managed to rise

I had to climb

I had to tell you my story

My story my seasons

Life changes

My struggles

My cries

My words

Revealed with pen and paper

Revealing me

The writer

The poet

And author

Sammy with pen

Sammy Pen that's me

The end of this chapter but life will throw you more pages.......

"Star"

Every child born is a star
The light glistens brightly into the universe, a trillion zillion miles away,
A buzz infinity and beyond
You are moving through light beyond your years
Your life will be your legacy

The fight through mud and dirt you are able to rise
Rise high above the expectations
The fight within you is your story
A legend here on earth
May your story not defeat your purpose

May you find it within to rise above it all
Gracefully take a bow
Applaud "Bravo"
Your name chanting on tongues across the globe and into the universe
May you begin a long due journey of finding who you truly are

Front and center stage
Perform
Rise you are great
Wishing you well to all your endeavors
Let the light within you guide you through

Salute to all the bright and gleaming stars!

EPILOGUE

The poet used an art form to convey her life experiences and feelings as a black woman in America who has experienced racism, discrimination, socio-economic barriers and challenges as well as injustice. Many of these challenges for marginalized people still exist today in modern society. While opportunities have been afforded to black and brown persons in America, discrimination, racism, exploitation and wage gap disparities, and injustice still are an issue for minorities today.

Throughout this anthology, readers' are able to critically analyze the black female experience in a time capsule throughout the years and decades through one black woman's experience from a teen to a black woman in America. While this time piece is not to segregate humans, it is intended to integrate humans through empathy and understanding of black and brown people and how we all shape society as a whole as well as the impacts.

ABOUT THE AUTHOR

Sammy Pen

Stay connected with Sammy Pen for upcoming books, and events. Go to Spotify and Amazon to checkout the playlist to this anthology. "CAN YOU HEAR ME FROM THE HILLS AND THE MOUNTAINS?" BY Sammy Pen

Willow Tree Books
www.willowtreebooks.com

Soon upcoming book releases
 "Them and Us" The Beginning and "Her Father's Ashes"

Social Media Connect
Instagram:sammypen_aka_ladysasha
Facebook: Sammy Pen

www.ingramcontent.com/pod-product-compliance
Lightning Source LLC
Chambersburg PA
CBHW020908100426
42737CB00045B/1049